The Last Lesbian Bar in the Midlands

Cleo Henry

First published in 2022 by Fourteen Publishing.
fourteenpoems.com

Design and typeset by Stromberg Design.
strombergdesign.co.uk

Proofreading and copy editing by Lara Kavanagh.
lk-copy.com

Printed by Print2Demand Ltd, Westoning, Bedfordshire, UK.

ISBN:
978-1-8383943-4-9

contents:

In Defence of Oyster / Lesbian Sex Metaphors

Not for the brine the shape
Not the straight actress
With her four identical limbs

But for the stench of a rock bottom tide
Yellow and gut warm for miles
Till it slams a hard blue sky

The long wade out to the oyster beds
Shells sheathed in silt cutting the shit
Out of pavement-soft soles

The beds pointing out to nothing
An unfurling hand
Full of pulsing cheeks

Achilles at the Dyke Bar

"If I remain embattled around the city of Troy
My homecoming dies but my fame will be eternal"
- The Iliad

blond curls cropped tight sticky with the wine-dark heat
of imagining what friends say when she's not there

some shot-pocked night or the ball of her thumb pinched
by a crab on fire island and she wept open mouthedly

look at beautiful Stu their pencil moustache babydoll lips
o yes she cried and cried these are heavy portents

to be crushed under and a blobfish only looks like that
because it was dredged up I'd look bad too we all would

caught out in the flickering dawn of music video autoplay
stroke my cheek nicely sing of me when I go get drinks

do tricks on the podium a dead seagull splutters revived
a sea urchin pulled new through a buttonhole's welt

daft orphan of time! completely undone by a salty breeze
bronze shells on a sandstrewn dancefloor look at Rex

marooned at the bar in their umpire's hat yes *she cried*
rubbery tears into the gutweed and we all gathered round

Arrangements

I knew this couple looking
for a third
their kitchen a stage
for the tablecloth trick
a flick of tooth-white fabric
leaving gleaming cutlery
hopeful palms of egg cups
trembling in the embarrassment of air

one or both of them
dream in oily nights
about ammonites of banknotes
unravelling to foam
their fruit bowl a brittle lifeboat
in a formica sea
when they wake they see
their partner's body
they think of polar bears adrift
in leaky rafts
but three
three could hold

(what's your name they ask his tiny head
who are you then)

I Hope I Never Learn

"Shucking 2,000 oysters a day at hog island"
string vest mesh
and a glove never looked so good

like that torso of Joe Brainard's like a postcard
from more fun than I've ever had certainly
and his beautiful face too
to farm something great in millions

like I never met a Simon I didn't like until
I did and he was a real shit but I still say it
often I've never met a Simon I didn't like
a total lie but
the faces of all those good
Simons happy little pansies they
look at me and I know
I'd eat a thousand clams
for one that kills me what
a classic idiot

Aetiology

and two blocks over someone's son is dead / a river is called after him / his name on a plaque 50 miles from where he died / burning cold / the sky is hibiscus red / when they dig him up / rebury him two blocks down from a dyke bar / called after someone's girlfriend / leather digs trenches / into sweaty shoulder skin / postered faces peel / into last month's shows / the bar closes when the meteorite hits / and still for months confused dykes stumble from the forest / to look at the crater / which is where we met / baby / locked eyes over tarred remains / of the first and last lesbian bar in the midlands / and dinosaur carcass / your curtain bangs singed / and millennia ahead of their time / I like to laugh against it / we tell this story so differently / like it wasn't two blocks from here / your fist was inside me / in a building condemned when / a chimney sweep skeleton clattered / to the ground-floor hearth / like a flash of laughing teeth / nothing dangerous / just a reminder of the whale we live in / who was probably called after somebody too / and two blocks over Lea DeLaria is on Conan / her B-U-T-C-H arm out / find the car keys find the car keys juuuuuudy garland / find the car keys find the car keys juuuuuudy garland / joan crawford / and that's how we learn / the strap of her wristwatch cuts through the air / time falling to either side of it / like an opening eye

Sonnet

Carson McCullers and I in Tesco
around us packets singing wowwowwow
at her sadness her death in Nyack New York
I feel butch as hell offering wildly
Carson McCullers this could all be ours
imagine this jam wounding your white shirt
filling our sink splattered on my bare leg
these frozen chips could last us a lifetime
her shaking head catches the yellow gleam
from gold bullions of American cheese
itching to melt and slough off its corners
melt as you would too Carson McCullers
without the cold air of the dairy aisle
this world clingfilmed for us this lightless light

Missed Connection at the Ruins of Gopsall's Folly Where Handel Maybe Wrote the Messiah (*though the folly wasn't built till long after) Overlooking Gopsall Hall (*now demolished)

ME: Some old tune, part goat part girl
(Nothing has existed at the same time)
YOU: Polished boots and almost whole

You roll in here, history's newest pearl
Carrying your quickness, your aspic shine
ME: Some old tune, part goat part girl

We make each roe's globe a private world
Our greedy eyes rubbed green with thyme
YOU: Polished boots and almost whole

We are just at the lip of this day's bowl
When your train screams in on its baited line
ME: Some old tune, part goat part girl

Take this bee, this sausage roll!
Your back is caked in city's grime!
YOU: Polished boots and almost whole

I watch another doric face unfurl
(Nothing has existed at the same time)
ME: Some old tune, part goat part girl
YOU: Polished boots and almost whole

A Solution Without a Problem

I want easy money / soft money /
third eyelid / baby's breath
money / I want money / that
holds me / money water / to
swim in / meetcute money / catch
my eye / make me feel young

like post it notes / born by
accident / a commercial failure /
till free samples / hit boise idaho
/ and each surface / a greedy
palimpsest / and the right amount
of bad / comes good / again

I only want / the train to take you
/ wherever I am / which is of
course / boise idaho / scabby skin
/ of potato fields / the second I
realise / I need something /
that sticks / but not quite / and

beyond idaho nothing / only / fur
lined money / in an edgeless
meadow / of green

Each Time I Piss on Hampstead Heath

I think about my ancestors,
all our various insides chucked outside
seeding a mottled grass.
I am a weathervane
scrabbling for north,
flapping over a knotted brow
of dense and serious roots.

Apparently, the park keeper, on seeing
the crucifix, the man up on it,
his bulging shorts and
the leather-trussed disciples crying
at his bleeding feet like black seals
basking on a darkened beach,
only said *clean up after yourselves.*

The morning found a hole
filled in and honest,
the men a fine and lifting mist.

In the bush's green guts I piss,
listening absently
to a distant birthday party,
thinking about who died and when
and what the soil keeps of them
and how Danaë got knocked up
by golden shower,

how surprised she must have been.
Imagine, me! A mother.

Lea DeLaria as Helen of Troy

if she was born a boat
she would look as good

amazing they found troy in her back garden
amazing what they found whole
a pomegranate hibiscus red
a filthy limerick carved
into blushing skin
still trembling

on the day she meant to turn it over
to the museum
lea delaria ate it

blood bright in the ash – after all
it was her garden
her blistered fist

Thot my last hour had come

- *After the rolodex of Samuel Steward*

Thot my last hour had come
But it hadn't I simply
Went home early a new man

My jaunty hat, new
My black eye, new
All new desires, also

I inform the street:
Good morning!
I was flayed alive!

Somewhere back there
Where I blew all
And all blew me

Where the body
Meets itself bloody
In a true deep sting

I was writhing about
Slimy and saw you –
You with your nice scarf

Dropping a rosy round future
Into my hands
Like a coin

When breakfast comes
You order in,
My tongue between your teeth

How New York's Butcher Girls Run Their Meat Omakase Subscription Service

The obvious thing to say would be Butcher Me but
Actually I want to be the only thing left entire

Mark out every other Wednesday for the rest of the year
To see your hard dyke hands blurring inside a ribcage

Only some have the right knives for the right jobs;
I want to see them slice through this poor image of a morning

Carve the slick-chained abattoir off its mainland roots,
Sail it clean by docks schismed from a paling sky

Cleave the rest: our friends, colleagues, all our mothers
Cleave yourselves, cleave each other, thumbed open like flies

That child you lift into the air too, I'm sorry
Feed me everything in its constituent parts

And leave me wholest, leave me a humming blade;
A gleaming curve in a world of cuts.

Distant Boats at Discos

'Put another way, we are not yet queer, but we can feel it as the warm illumination of a horizon'

- *José Esteban Muñoz*

Beyond our heads licked wet by the bar's coarse tongue

And our plum drunk bodies, dancing hard and buckle struck,

The sightline heaves with boats, the whole horizon a jostling harbour.

The stacks' rough breath rubs the tacky ceiling grey

Leaves traces of itself for weeks in our good shoes' laces.

A drag king's strap keels to the boats' north stars, a bright rubber sundial

Telling us all where to look, when to look there, each smear of light

Returned to us fourfold by the discoball flanks of holiday paddle steamers.

Bruised blue by fresh denim two bulldykes go home together,

Practise together longshoremanship, the hauling in, the long looks west.

West is where the boats look too, dreaming of all-American road trips in the surf,

A letter marked 'flee, all is discovered' the only thing left in a
wind-bitten hold.

I believe this is what all crossroads end up looking like, the last lit
part

of an emptying town, a party with its ear tuned to a distant fog
horn-

Their brushed steel cries are our cries, their delayed departure our
own

And beyond them only more horizons, each lapping the fringe of
the last like a morning.

I Love How Americans Talk About Their Towns Almost as Much as I Miss You

It's how they say the name and then the state,
Boulder Colorado, like they are daring you
to mythologise a place because you've never been

or you went once and the food was good
or you liked the way the ground
ate the sun like a lover's thumb.

If I was a town I'd be Thebes;
I've never eaten fruit without picturing it
on someone else's coat of arms.

But your name sits under the cloche
of a crystal-cut sea. Your streets empty,
the hollow bowl of your marketplace.

It's sad but when you see a myth too close up
it just becomes a story you tell about yourself
and what then? The comfort being that

for the names we can't carry any further
down the road, we know the water is there
to rush in and fill the gaps.

Tipping Point

This nun is absolutely shredding
her wimple (latex) gleams in the sun (grey)
skateboard kicking over God's concrete brow
thigh slit grinning to high heaven

I'd ask her to pray for me
just to have me in mind
whilst she brushes her teeth
clicks her rosary
punches out nerds
just to be there
where she is
the tipping point to grace

The Record

What do you remember?

It was me and Cynthia Nixon,
After she ran for Governor but before
The airing of *And Just Like That* in which
She revisits her iconic character
Miranda Hobbes from *Sex and the City.*

Governor of what?

Of New York. She was still mad
With the blood of the race and wept
When we reached the pit.

Which pit was it?

The pit with all of New York
At the bottom of it, gleaming
Like a freshly punched face.

What could you see?

Not much. The navels
Of a few small fires.
A couple of guys
Jerking each other off.
Some snail shells.

What did you do there?

Cynthia was beside herself,
Crying a lot
And pointing out bits of sidewalk

From under a dyke bar's awning
From her wedding day
From her first onscreen kiss
With David Eigenberg-
All in the slick melee
Of soho's smashed ass.

I did the same although
I never actually went.

Who is David Eigenberg?

You might know him as Steve,
A bartender.

Do you know him?

I don't know anybody in New York at all
Which is, actually, romantic.

And were you the attacker or the attacked?

I don't know. I can't remember.

How can you not remember?

It was dark and I was alone.

What about Cynthia Nixon?

She had gone by then.

How can we know for sure you were there?

You can smell it on me,
If you'd like. If you'd like,
Come to the pit with me. Like me,
Lose three of your good teeth
To the pit. If that's what you want.

I don't want that.

Well what I want is to be alive only
As the footprints of a killer are alive
To be touched by a gloved hand
And told, firmly, where I've just been.

You look terrible today

I know.

I'm sorry I dragged you here, away from your lunch

You had to be sure.

I did, you are always almost vanished
Just beyond where my throwing arm can reach
On a good day and with the right wind

You're always doing that, note it
For the recording-
That you do that a lot.

Thanks and Acknowledgements

A few phrases from these poems were borrowed or inspired by other works.
"I Hope I Never Learn" quotes the title of the Munchies YouTube video *Shucking 2,000 Oysters a Day at Hog Island.*
"Aetiology" borrows and adapts words from Lea DeLaria's 2014 appearance on Conan O'Brien's Late Night Show.
"Thot my last hour had come" takes its title and quotes from Samuel Steward's *Stud Files*, as found in *Secret Historian* by Justin Spring.
"How New York's Butcher Girls Run Their Meat Omakase Subscription Service" takes its title from the Eater YouTube video of the same name.
The epigraph of "Achilles at the Dyke Bar" is taken from the *Iliad,* translated by Cleo Henry.
The epigraph of "Distant Boats at Discos" is taken from José Esteban Muñoz's *Cruising Utopia.*

Thanks to the publications in which some of these poems have previously appeared: *Ambit, T'Art Magazine, Banshee Press, The Selkie, Colliding Lines,* and *Broken Sleep Books.*

Huge thanks to Ben Townley-Canning for the words of encouragement over the years, and for editing and publishing this collection – it means a huge amount.

Thank you to Cafe Rustique for hosting and caffeinating me whilst I wrote much of this collection.

For your irreplaceable conversation and inspiration, thank you Emma, Ali, Charlotte, Rhys, and Tom.

Thank you to my parents for your support and Pub Dog for your enthusiasm.

And, of course, Alex – you're a dream to me.